The Fat Dog
And other poems

Sineidin O'Niall

Copyright © 2017 Sineidin O'Niall

All rights reserved.

ISBN: 978-0-9913801-8-3

DEDICATION

Dedicated with love to Elfers and Willow and to Pumpkin and Tippy and Bounce, to Penny and Toby, to Pantouffe and Sketch, Bird and Ptoo, Paco, Bungey, Pan, Parker, and Puff
and to everyone who has ever loved a furry, feathered, or fluffy friend.

CONTENTS

The Fat Dog	1
In Rehearsal	16
Arguing With Air	17
Playing Fiddle on a Saturday Morning	20
Staying in Touch	22
The Swan Head Boat	24
Being Content	25
Encounter	26
Love Hurts	27
Aliens	28
Waiting for the Microwave	32
Tide os Out in the Studio	33
Songs From a Fog Bound Sea	34
About the Author	36

THE FAT DOG

She was a very small puppy
and very alone
Her world was a cardboard box
Where she was kept, but not loved.

One morning she felt her box wobble
and fly and pitch and roll
She stayed where she was
Until it stopped.

There she was, tiny and alone
On her hind legs
peaking over the edge of her world
in front of a grocery store

A stranger came and hugged her
and picked her up and carried her away
to a new home
With someone who loved her.

She learned to explore
Fields and skies and flowers and stars
Trees and lawns and comets and kids
So many wonderful things to see

Flower Dog

New foods and spices, and critters big and small
messages on fence posts and tales in the wind
So many smells complex and enticing.
Each day was a day of adventure
and discovery of places beyond beyond.

Wind Dog

In her home when she was small
she loved a cat and loved her yard
and slept at night in her own wooden bed
where she could watch the cat watching over her

Night Dog

She grew and raced along the banks
of deep and mysterious rivers
She jumped and ran between towering redwoods
and played in blowing drifts of cottonwood seeds.

She grew as big a dog as she would be
She went to school and tried,
but there was only one person she would obey
Her friend, her companion, her heart

Then one day another dog came home
A bassett.puppy with short short legs
And long long ears
Too small to fear and too loving not to love.

Earth Dog

They were the three
The cat, the puppy and she.
They played together, walked together.
ate together and slept together.

She and her puppy played in the water,
chased pigeons at the park,
wrestled on the grass
and were always together.

Together, she and her puppy walked in the desert
through saguaro and ocotillo
Together they breathed the desert sickness
and only she survived.

She grew old with her person and her cat
They chased the wind in mountain passes
and ran from waves on Pacific shores
They looked at the lights of starry nights beside
campfires in the forest

Fire Dog

Now she is old and has lost her sight.
Her cat went away and she sleeps alone
She can't walk well and has gotten fat.
She lies In her small wooden bed, and nowhere else.

She is happy though.
Perhaps now, more than ever,
she is happy in her small wooden bed
She imagines and remembers.

In her mind she sees the cat watch over her
and her puppy at her side
She imagines the wind, and the stars, and the night,
and the flowers and the trees and fields

She remembers the rivers, the ocean,
The desert, the waves, the warm fires,
She remembers running and jumping and wrestling
She knows she has been, and is, loved.

Water Dog

The Fat Dog is old and crippled
The Fat Dog is blind,
But the Fat dog is happy and all is well.
Today the Fat Dog is everything she imagines.

In Rehearsal

Ever so small,
and ever so old,
She moves around
the circle of the dance.

Thinking,
always thinking,
She counts the beats
and walks the steps.

Looking,
always looking,
She goes from
each face to the next.

Waiting.
gently waiting,
She hopes for
that small glance of kindness,

and appreciation.

Arguing With Air

Please scan your first item.
Hold on, let me get my things out of my bag
Unexpected item in the bagging area. Please remove before continuing
That's my bag. I TOLD you I had a bag.
Unexpected item in the bagging area, Please remove before continuing
Ok ok, there I removed my bag.
Unexpected item in the bagging area, Please wait for assistance.

Please scan your first item
Ok, ok, OK there
Four ninety-five
What? No, the sign said two for six dollars
Do you want to delete this item?
No, I just want to pay the marked price
Do you want to delete this item?
Ok, fine, delete it. I don't need it anyway
Please wait for assistance

Please scan your first item
Ok, here …. here … here …….. scan damn you
Six ninety-nine
What? Oh, ok
Ninety-nine ………………….. cents
Ninety-nine ………………….. cents
Ninety-nine ………………….. cents
What? I only got two.

Do you want to delete this item
Damn right
Please wait for assistance.

Please check your cart for additional items
I told you, I brought a bag
Please check your cart for additional items
There are no additional items
Please check your cart for additional items
I CHECKED… it's a great fucking void of nothing

Please insert cash or press pay with card
Hold on, hold on let me get my money out
Please insert cash or press pay with card
It's stuck, my pants are too tight
Please insert cash or press pay with card
wait
Please insert cash or press pay with card
Shut up
Please insert cash or press pay with card

There, that's five dollars
Please insert cash or press pay with card
I'm going as fast as I can, damn you
Please insert cash or press pay with card
Ok, here, here, here's a twenty
Please insert cash or press pay with card
Oh for Christ's sake give me a second will you
Please insert cash or press pay with card

There, that's my last five now let me out of here
Unexpected item in the bagging area
What? Are you kidding? I told you I had a bag.
Unexpected item in the bagging area
I told you … it's MY DAMN BAG
Unexpected item in the bagging area
It's not unexpected you idiot, just give me my damn change
Unexpected item in the bagging area
Shut up, just shut up
Please wait for assistance.

Please remove your items from the bagging area.
Shut up
Please remove your items from the bagging area.
Shut up
Please remove your items from the bagging area.
Shut up
Please remove your items from the bagging area.
There, I'm done
Please remove your items from the bagging area.
Shut up

Thank you for shopping at Save Mart.

Playing Fiddle on a Saturday Morning

Standing on a pebble walkway
So many shades of grey
White grey
Graphite grey
Charcoal grey
and I with my fiddle.

Music for a sunny morning:
a strathspey
a march
an air.
A blue jay ran along the edge of my vision.

A pebble walkway
So many patterns of grey
Returning from the jay
a new grey pattern at my feet
Complex and precise, it flutters
(Was it the wind?)

Intricate patterns
of grey and white
Then, slowly
(Was it the wind?)
It unfolds to bright colors
Of orange, and black, and yellow

At my feet
A flutter
A slow fanning
(Was it the wind?)
Patterns of grey beauty
Patterns of color

And so I played to it
With all the feeling I could convey
Happy jigs, polkas, and hornpipes
Loving airs and Massanet
And it waved (was it the wind?)
Until it waved no more.

Playing for a dying butterfly.
Now lying quiet
and beautiful
and still
on the pebbles
at my feet.

Staying in Touch

There is a piece of paper
folded
in an envelope
in a file
in a box
in storage

It used to be love
Now it's a symbol

There was a time
when touch was all.
We were inseparable
and probably annoying.

Even when we parted
we swore we'd always be friends
we talked at least
daily

When distance came
we wrote
daily
then weekly
then ….
One last time

There is a piece of paper
folded
in an envelope
in a file
in a box
in storage

I last saw it
48 years ago

but I know
it's there.

Sineidin O'Niall

The Swan Head Boat

Stand on the shore and look within
the wraiths of mist that stroke the sands.
See what was and what might be
and hold the sight with children's eyes.

Black rocks shape the sea's cold breath
as it exhales to the shores.
From out the mist, the swan head boat
moves and lifts with silent oars.

Small birds hop from kelp to shell,
A fog horn tolls the waves and sea,
the bell buoy mourns the loss of time,
while shadows speak of what could be.

The cormorants wait in grim formation
on rocks above the waters' spinning
to listen to the passing time
and watch the old beginning.

I am young again and whole
quietly in love with the sea
standing on that far away shore
in the place I want to be.

The swan head boat that carried my heart
rocks with the waves and the sea
and glides to a place I've never been
and a peace I'll never see.

Stand as fog enshrouds the beach
the swan boat lifts and turns
it dissolves into the mist
and to the fog returns.

Being Content

Lying in bed.
Cat curled up at my feet and
dog stretched out at my hip
his head on my stomach
rising and falling
with each breath.

Snow falling outside the window
and the wind
singing in the eaves.

When the wind stops
there is no sound at all

except

the gentle sound of purring
and the distant sound of surf.

A quiet kind of happiness

Encounter

The tide is quiet in the morning.
A single gull cries into
the last wisps of fog.

She steps carefully
From one rock to another.
Her yellow parka has a hood
rimmed with fur
pulled up over her head.

The air is still in the morning.
A seal lion calls to
hush the laplets on the shore.

He walks down the pier breathing
the clean smells of a new day.
His jeans are worn
and stained
with paint.

The shore is peaceful in the morning.
Three otters splash
and dive beneath the silent swell.

She places her leather boots with care
and ascends to the highest rock.
As he passes below her
He hears her hiss to the morning,
"I'll be glad when he's dead."

The tide is quiet in the morning.
The gulls cry, the waves lap, the seal lion calls
and as he walks away he hears behind,
"I'll be glad when he's dead."

Love Hurts

My cat is black
And orange
Named after a lost boy
She can fly
Just for the joy of flying

Curled on my lap
She hums
Liked a muted wash board
And kneads me with her paws
Five needle sharp claws
Then five more

Love hurts.

Aliens

They call them "aliens".
The quiet workers who
tend to our food
so others can eat
and fear them.

Green and yellow, pink and navy,
orange and baby blue
they work bent over, moving slowly
down the row
picking strawberries.

I wonder if I could stand
the pain, the monotony
the cold, the wet, the heat,
day after day, month after month
year after year.

Each is hooded, each wears a mask
and each is bundled against
the early morning mist as
they crouch and bend
harvesting lettuce

I wonder if I would
be brave enough,
stoic enough, or strong enough
to endure.

Why do they do it?
How do they endure aching muscles,
tired limbs, and numbed senses
for a few dollars to send home
miles away?

They burst from the reeds
in the dry river bed.
Twenty runners.
Some carry cardboard suitcases,
some hold hands.

Men and women, not one is younger than forty.
They run looking over their shoulders.
Looking back, they run across the dry river bed road.
The first disappear
back into the reeds

Falling behind, a woman trips and falls.
Her suitcase breaks open.
She wears a bright print dress.
It once was pretty, but now it's worn
and so is she.

Back out of the reeds A man runs with a limp.
He lifts her to her feet so carefully, So lovingly
I'm envious
as they hurry into the reeds,
the suitcase left behind.

The runners are gone
the wind whispers
and rustles the reeds
a bird sings
feathered seeds dance in the heat

Roaring and spinning wheels
two green jeeps fly over the river bank,
and grind circles in the sand.
Anonymous hunters.

I wonder if I have
the strength of spirit
to live in flight
for the sake of love
of the ones I left behind?

Spider holes, they're called spider holes
where they sleep at night.
Dug into the ground in the hills
hidden from the sight
of anonymous hunters.

The spider holes are invisible
shelters against the cold night,
unless the sides collapse
and become a secret grave
and tomb.

Could I endure the terrors

of a land in which
language locks me out
and hates me for who I am
for the sake of my daughter?

Is it despair or bravery that spurs them on?
Is it desperation or determination
that brings them here?
Is it fear or ignorance
that tries to drive them away?

There's so little I know
about myself.

Waiting for the Microwave

Almost zen like
Cleansing breath
Empty your mind
Focus your chi
The hum becomes one with om

Breathe in
(Two minutes and forty-three seconds still?)
Breathe out
Focus on nothingness
(Two minutes and twenty-four seconds? Really?)

Feel the hunger
Become one with the hunger
Breathe in
Move your energy to Dantian
(1 minute fifty-two seconds)

Visualize ocean breezes
Breathe out
Find the space behind your eyes
Go to the ding
(Come on, finish. One minute twelve seconds?)

Damn ding better come soon
or I'm going to eat it frozen
That's the problem with damn technology
You can't count on it at all
I'll bet the stupid microwave isn't even … ding

Tide is Out in the Studio

Tide is out in the studio
at the glass table looking out at the sea
where paintings sometimes come to life
the rocks of jars,
the tubes of paint
the flotsam of brushes
and pencils
are left exposed on the beach of glass.

Tide is out in the studio
tubes of paints once separated
are now intermingled
tubes of red with blue
and black with green
and brown with purple
exposed on the beach of the glass

Tide is out in the studio
the shadow place of imagination
where pictures bloom, and fade
hills and people
sun and trees
laughter and despair
and Brandenburg 3 on the floor.

Songs From A Fogbound Sea

Before the colors of day
or after the Dies Irae
of an empty life
there is the sea
the fogbound sea

Under the horrors
and over the tremors
of the shifting world
there is the shore
of a fog bound sea

Blinded by the glare
deafened by the cries
of strangers in pain
There is music calling
from the fog bound sea

Go to the shore
kneel on the sand
feel the embrace
and the endless grey
of the fog bound sea

Wavelets set the quiet rhythm
shifting swells the beat
seaweed and the sleeping birds
send harmonies of healing
 with quiet songs

from the fogbound sea.

The Fat Dog and other poems

About the Author

Sineidin O'Niall was born in the spring of 1949 in Dallas, Texas, but grew up in California. During her school years she was a competitive swimmer, learned to play viola, and became slightly fanatical about Pacific intertidal invertebrates.

After high school she alternated between living "on the road" and getting a college degree. In the process, she worked as a motel maid, pizza cook, professional sailing crew and sailboat salesperson, advertising and television show writer, stuntwoman, sanitarium attendant, dormitory housekeeper, church cleaning lady, mortuary attendant, carpet mill worker, tour guide, movie extra, apartment painter, and swimming instructor.

In later years she was a teacher and professional musician. As a studio and performing artist she played viola in several orchestras and performed in live shows with artists such as Gordon MacRae, Sammy Davis Jr., George Benson, Smokey Robinson, and Vincent Price.

Eventually Sineidin O'Niall ended up practicing law for almost 30 years as both a successful trial and appellate attorney in State and Federal Courts.

Most recently the road called her name once again and she packed her two cats and one fluffy dog into a van and headed east.

She now lives in Lubec, Maine where she is enjoying a dramatic lack of success as an artist and Celtic fiddler.

The Fat Dog and other poems

www.ingramcontent.com/pod-product-compliance
Lightning Source LLC
Chambersburg PA
CBHW041743040426

42444CB00001B/5